T0306621

Kid's Box

New Generation

British English

Caroline Nixon &
Michael Tomlinson

CAMBRIDGE

Activity Book
with Digital Pack

3

Thanks and Acknowledgements

Authors' thanks

Many thanks to everyone at Cambridge University Press and Assessment for their dedication and hard work, and in particular to:

Liane Grainger and Lynn Townsend for supervising the whole project and guiding us calmly through the storms.

We would also like to thank all our pupils and colleagues, past, present and future, at Star English academy in Murcia, especially Jim Kelly for his friendship and support throughout the years.

Zara Hutchinson-Goncalves for her energy, enthusiasm and expertise. Thanks for doing such a great job.

Dedications

For the women who were my pillars of strength when I most needed it: Milagros Marin, Sara de Alba, Elia Navarro and Maricarmen Balsalobre. – CN

To Pablo and Carlota. This one's for you. Kid's Box's biggest fans. – MT

The authors and publishers acknowledge the following sources of copyright material and are grateful for the permissions granted. While every effort has been made, it has not always been possible to identify the sources of all the material used, or to trace all copyright holders. If any omissions are brought to our notice, we will be happy to include the appropriate acknowledgements on reprinting and in the next update to the digital edition, as applicable.

Key: U = Unit

Photography

The following photos are sourced from Getty Images.

U1: Nickbeer/iStock/Getty Images Plus; clubfoto/iStock/Getty Images Plus; SW Productions/Photodisc; Halfpoint/iStock/Getty Images Plus; Geber86/E+; Westend61; Halfpoint/iStock/Getty Images Plus; Comstock/Stockbyte; Adene Sanchez/E+; Prostock-Studio/iStock/Getty Images Plus; Johner Images; PeopleImages/iStock/Getty Images Plus; Maskot; Cavan Images; Thomas Barwick/DigitalVision; Aleksandr Zubkov/Moment; enjoynz/DigitalVision Vectors; LuckyTD/iStock/Getty Images Plus; Cyndi Monaghan/Moment; John M Lund Photography Inc/Stone; John M Lund Photography Inc/Stone; **U2:** vernonwiley/E+; Sally Anscombe/Moment; SerrNovik/iStock/Getty Images Plus; Stuart Ashley/DigitalVision; monkeybusinessimages/iStock/Getty Images Plus; Daisy-Daisy/iStock/Getty Images Plus; Marc Romanelli; noblige/iStock/Getty Images Plus; Sino Images/500px Asia; Alistair Berg/DigitalVision; FatCamera/iStock/Getty Images Plus; robertprzybysz/iStock/Getty Images Plus; **U3:** baona/iStock/Getty Images Plus; alphaspirit/iStock/Getty Images Plus **U4:** Westend61; Alex Potemkin/E+; Ilona Nagy/Moment; **U5:** Mike Hill/stone; Digital Vision; Moussa81/iStock/Getty Images Plus; ozgurcankaya/E+; DaniloAndjus/E+; AlesVeluscek/E+; Westend61; dejan Jekic/iStock/Getty Images Plus; Cavan Images; Richard Hutchings/Corbis Documentary; **U6:** Yuichiro Chino/Moment; solarisimages/iStock/Getty Images Plus; bamlou/DigitalVision Vectors; Kwanchai Lerttanapunyaporn/EyeEm; juststock/iStock/Getty Images Plus; mbortolino/E+; skegbydave/E+; Jose Luis Pelaez Inc/DigitalVision; TonyBaggett/iStock/Getty Images Plus; jayk7/Moment; 3alexd/iStock/Getty Images Plus; MoMo Productions/DigitalVision; Kraig Scarbinsky/DigitalVision; imtmphoto/iStock/Getty Images Plus; Kkolosov/iStock/Getty Images Plus; Larissa Veronesi/Moment; Image Source; skynesher/E+; George Doyle/Stockbyte; Fuse/Corbis; Ihor Bulyhin/iStock/Getty Images Plus; Julie Toy/Stone; Seamind Panadda/EyeEm; Rubberball/Mike Kemp/Brand X Pictures; Studio Paggy; Vukasin Ormanovic/EyeEm; Jose Luis Pelaez Inc/DigitalVision; dblight/iStock/Getty Images Plus; Nick David/DigitalVision; Peter Dazeley/Photodisc; JGI; **U7:** bikec/E+; 1001slide/E+; Lysandra Cook/Moment; mallardg500/Moment; Kyrin Geisser/EyeEm; by wildestanimal/Moment; Mike Hill/Stone; Don White/E+; John W Banagan/Photodisc; James Warwick/The Image Bank; Andrea Edwards/EyeEm; Kathrin Raedel/EyeEm;

Brian Mckay Photography/Moment; Bruno Guerreiro/Moment; dottedhippo/iStock/Getty Images Plus; Paul Starosta/Stone; Somedaygood/iStock/Getty Images Plus; R. Andrew Odum/Photodisc; cinoby/E+; hakule/E+; Dorling Kindersley; **U8:** Christine Müller/EyeEm; wiratgasem/Moment; Mint Images/Mint Images RF; clubfoto/iStock/Getty Images Plus; Alexandra Lorenz/iStock/Getty Images Plus Santiaga/iStock/Getty Images Plus; Piotr Marcinski/EyeEm; lenazap/E+; Westend61; Yutthana Chumkhot/EyeEm; Ultima_Gaina/iStock Editorial; tatyana_tomsickova/iStock/Getty Images Plus; Lane Oatey/Blue Jean Images; Jupiterimages/Stockbyte; Nerthuz/iStock/Getty Images Plus; Avalon/Universal Images Group; Yevgen Romanenko/Moment; milanfoto/iStock/Getty Images Plus; Preto_perola/iStock/Getty Images Plus; Mutlu Kurtbas/E+; Tomekbudujedomek/Moment; macroworld/E+; Sohel Parvez Haque/EyeEm; Jeffrey Coolidge/Stone; tatyana_tomsickova/iStock/Getty Images Plus; Lane Oatey/Blue Jean Images; **V01:** Drazen_/E+; PeopleImages/iStock/Getty Images Plus; kirin_photo/iStock/Getty Images Plus; **V02:** izusek/E+; MachineHeadz/iStock/Getty Images Plus; Jupiterimages/Goodshoot; **V03:** kilukilu/iStock/Getty Images Plus; Imgorthand/E+; Nick Dolding/Photodisc; Kittkavin Kao Ien/EyeEm; **V04:** Kasipat Phonlamai/EyeEm; marugod83/iStock/Getty Images Plus; SelectStock/Vetta. Daly and Newton/The Image Bank; BunnyHollywood/E+; Sollina Images; Stephen Simpson/Stone; andresr/E+; BraunS/E+; FatCamera/E+; vgajic/E+; Motortion/iStock/Getty Images Plus; DGLimages/iStock/Getty Images Plus; wilpunt/E+; Westend61; DiMaggio/Kalish/The Image Bank; Werner Dieterich; Valerie Loiseleux/iStock/Getty Images Plus;

Commissioned photography by Copy cat and Trevor Clifford Photography.

Illustrations

Antonio Cuesta; Carol Herring (The Bright Agency); Leo Trinidad (The Bright Agency); Marek Jagucki; Michael McCabe (Beehive)

Cover Illustration by Pronk Media Inc.

Audio

Audio production by Creative listening.

Video

Video acknowledgements are in the Teacher Resources on Cambridge One.

Design and typeset

Blooberry Design

Additional authors

Katy Kelly: Lock's Sounds and spelling

Rebecca Legros: geography, maths, science and music sections

Freelance editor

Carolyn Wright

Contents

 1 Read and complete the sentences.

> reading   ~~name's~~   I'm   nine   sister   comic

Hello. My name's Suzy Star. I'm five. I've got a dog. She's called Dotty.

a Hello. My _name's_ Stella Star. I'm _____ . I've got a brother and a _____ .

b Hi. _____ Simon Star. I'm eight. I like _____ comics. This is my favourite _____ .

 2 Now draw and write about you.

Hi. My name's _____ .
I'm _____ .
I've got a _____ .
_____ called _____ .
I like _____ .
This is my favourite _____ .

Me!

Language: introductions   ⬛ Do the online activities on **Practice Extra** as you complete this unit

1 Look and colour.

twenty – grey   thirteen – yellow   twelve – black
ten – brown   eighteen – red   eleven – pink
fourteen – white   nineteen – blue   fifteen – green

2 🎧 2 Listen and write.

1 _____ 14 kites _____   5 _____
2 _____   6 _____
3 _____   7 _____
4 _____   8 _____

Match and write.

1

Simon

Simon
Meera

2

Stella
Lenny

3

Suzy
Alex

4

5

6

2 Now answer the questions.

> No, he isn't.   ~~Yes, he is.~~   Yes, she is.
> No, she isn't.   Yes, he is.   No, she isn't.

1 Is Simon playing a computer game?   Yes, he is.
2 Is Stella painting?
3 Is Lenny playing badminton?
4 Is Suzy reading?
5 Is Meera riding a bike?
6 Is Alex reading a comic?

 Read and match.

1 Is Lily reading?
2 Where's the kite?
3 Have you got a sister?
4 Is Jim eating?
5 What's Daisy eating?

a No, he's drinking.
b No, I've got a brother.
c She's eating an ice cream.
d It's under the bed.
e Yes. She loves books.

Language: present continuous

Read, write and colour.

Jane, Fred, Vicky, Paul, Sally, Beth and Zak are in the park now. Sally's riding a black bike. Fred's flying a big orange kite. Beth's playing football with a small brown dog. The dog's getting the purple ball. Zak's sitting with a fat grey dog. Vicky likes dogs. She's taking photographs with a green camera. Paul's playing hockey with his cousin, Jane. She's wearing a new yellow T-shirt and old blue jeans.

 Look at the picture. Correct the sentences.

1 Paul's flying a kite.
   No. Fred's flying a kite.

2 Beth's got a camera.

3 Zak's playing hockey.

4 Vicky's got a bike.

5 Fred and Sally have got dogs.

6 Jane's getting the ball.

Lock's sounds and spelling

1 Say and write.

spider	nine	~~eight~~
five	late	play
paint	drive	~~white~~
grey	bike	kite
train	plane	like

/aɪ/
white

/eɪ/
eight

2 Complete the words with the letters.

1 F i v e sp i d e rs are jumping.   e / i / i / e
2 Can you pl ____ the piano?   y / a
3 We've got a b __ k __ and a gr ____ car.   i / y / e / e
4 I l __ k __ eating sandwiches and c __ k __ .   i / e / e / a
5 ____ ght girls are p ____ nting.   e / i / i / a

3 Read and complete the table.

My friends are called Peter and Daisy. Peter can ride a bike, but he can't swim. He can play the piano and he can play badminton. Daisy can ride a bike, swim and play the piano. She can't play badminton.

Name	Peter	Daisy
Ride a bike		✓
Swim	✗	
Play the piano		
Play badminton		

Now write about your friends.

My friends _____

_____

_____

1 🎧 3 **Listen and join.**

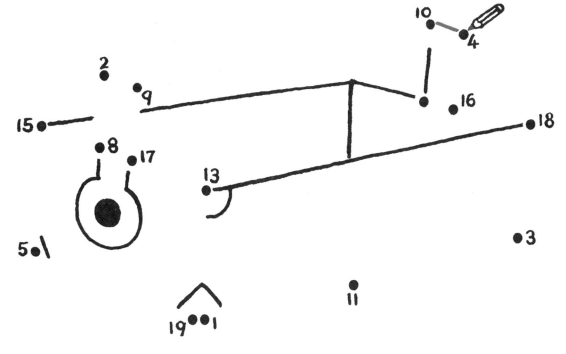

What's this? _____

2 **Complete and answer.**

1 What's your favourite comic? _____

2 What's your favourite toy? _____

3 What's your favourite sport? _____

4 What's your favourite colour? _____

5 What's your favourite animal? _____

6 What's your favourite _____ ? _____

1 Family matters

2 Look at Activity 1 and complete the sentences.

son   daughter   parents   granddaughters
aunt   ~~grandparents~~   uncle   grandson

1 The people on the bus are Stella's ___grandparents___ .
2 Grandma Star's _____ is on the bike.
3 The girls in the boat are Grandpa Star's _____ .
4 The woman in the helicopter is Grandma Star's _____ .
5 The boy on the bike is Mr Star's _____ .
6 Suzy's _____ is in the lorry.
7 The people in the plane are Stella's _____ .
8 Simon's _____ is in the helicopter.

📱 Do the online activities on **Practice Extra** as you complete this unit

Who is speaking? Read and write 'a' or 'b'.

> **a** Grandma and Grandpa Star **b** Stella, Simon and Suzy

1 Uncle Fred is our uncle.   [b]
2 Simon is our grandson.   [ ]
3 Grandma and Grandpa Star are our grandparents.   [ ]
4 Suzy and Stella are our granddaughters.   [ ]
5 Aunt May is our aunt.   [ ]

 Read and complete the sentences.

The Star family are doing different things. Suzy's in the living room. She's drawing a picture of her Uncle Fred. He's sleeping on the sofa. Simon's in the garden. He's playing tennis with his Aunt May. She loves playing tennis with him because he's very good at sport. Stella's got a new camera and she's taking a photo of her grandparents in the dining room. The children's parents are in the kitchen. They're making dinner.

1 The Star ___family___ are doing different things.
2 Suzy's drawing a picture of her _____.
3 Uncle Fred's _____ on the sofa.
4 Simon and his _____ are in the garden.
5 Simon's very _____ at sport.
6 Stella's taking a photo of her _____.
7 Grandma and Grandpa Star are in the _____.
8 The children's _____ are in the kitchen.

Read and circle the best answer.

1 Suzy: Do you enjoy shopping?
  Uncle Fred: a) I've got a new T-shirt.
  b) (No, I don't.)

2 Suzy: Does Grandma like painting?
  Uncle Fred: a) Yes, I do.
  b) Yes, she loves painting.

3 Suzy: Does Stella want to be a doctor?
  Uncle Fred: a) Yes, she does.
  b) Yes, she can.

4 Suzy: Do you enjoy playing tennis?
  Uncle Fred: a) Yes, he does.
  b) No, but Aunt May enjoys it.

5 Suzy: Does Dotty like having a bath?
  Uncle Fred: a) No, she doesn't.
  b) She loves swimming.

6 Suzy: Do you want to ride your bike?
  Uncle Fred: a) Yes, I do.
  b) Simon's riding his bike.

Look and match the sentences.

1 Uncle Fred's got a bike.
2 Grandpa's got a camera.
3 Simon's got a ball.
4 Mr Star's got a guitar.
5 Stella's got a book.
6 Grandma's got some eggs.

a She wants to read it.
b He wants to take a photo.
c She wants to make a cake.
d He wants to play it.
e He wants to ride it.
f He wants to play basketball.

Language: present simple

1 Find and write the words.

w	r	t	s	o	l	m	n	a	s	t	i
q	u	i	e	t	o	p	a	r	b	a	n
e	g	i	h	o	s	c	u	r	l	y	h
d	u	k	e	s	s	a	g	e	s	r	k
f	u	n	n	y	a	c	h	e	m	u	l
v	a	r	t	y	o	l	t	i	k	y	c
e	g	h	f	p	o	e	y	s	o	v	s
b	x	r	a	t	b	v	g	a	l	t	d
m	c	h	i	l	b	e	a	r	d	c	a
s	a	s	r	s	t	r	a	i	g	h	t

1 elvcre   clever
2 haynugt
3 utqei
4 rebad
5 unyfn
6 lucyr
7 gittshra
8 aifr

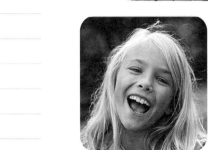

2 Ask and answer. Complete the table.

Do you enjoy singing?

Yes, I do. ✓

No, I don't. ✗

Do you enjoy …	♫ singing?	🎲 playing games?	_____?	_____?

Lock's sounds and spelling

1 **Look and write.**

1 Mother is drinking
   water .

3 I love eating
   _____ .

2 My father is a
   _____ .

4 Her brother likes playing
   _____

   games.

2 **Write the missing letters.**

1 My broth _e_ _r_ loves eating burg _e_ _r_ s.   (true) / false
2 The farm _____ wants to eat dinn _____ .   true / false
3 There's a bus driv _____ playing with a tig _____ .   true / false
4 The teach _____ likes painting post _____ s.   true / false
5 My sist _____ loves swimming in the riv _____ .   true / false
6 My moth _____ is working on the comput _____ .   true / false

3 **Look and circle 'true' or 'false'.**

1 🎧 5 🐵 **Listen and colour and write. There is one example.**

How big is your family?

1 **How many people are in your extended family? Count and write.**

Grandparents: _____
Aunts: _____
Uncles: _____
Cousins: _____
Total: _____

2 **Complete and answer.**

1 How many aunts and uncles have you got?
(_____ aunts + _____ uncles)

2 Which is greater, the number of aunts, or the number of uncles?
(_____ aunts _____ uncles)

3 How many ears have all your grandparents got?
(2 ears x _____ grandparents = _____ ears)

4 How many toes have your cousins got?
(10 toes x _____ cousins = _____ toes)

3 **Guess and measure. Complete the table.**

	Guess!	Measure!
	_____ cm	_____ cm
	_____ cm	_____ cm
	_____ cm	_____ cm
	_____ cm	_____ cm

Maths: measuring | 🛡 critical thinking

Do you remember?

1 🎧 6 **Listen and colour and write. There is one example.**

2 **Write the answers.**

1 What does the thief look like?

_____

2 What is the thief wearing?

_____

3 Who is in the park?

_____

4 Who do you think is sitting on the bench next to the cat?

_____

5 Why does Lock think that the woman is the thief?

_____

6 Why is the woman angry?

_____

2 Home sweet home

1 Match. Write the words.

1 fl
2 li
3 ba
4 do
5 st

flat
floor
_____
_____
_____
_____

reet
wnstairs
airs
sement
ve
at
or
oor
ft
lcony

2 Complete the crossword.

Down ↓   Across →

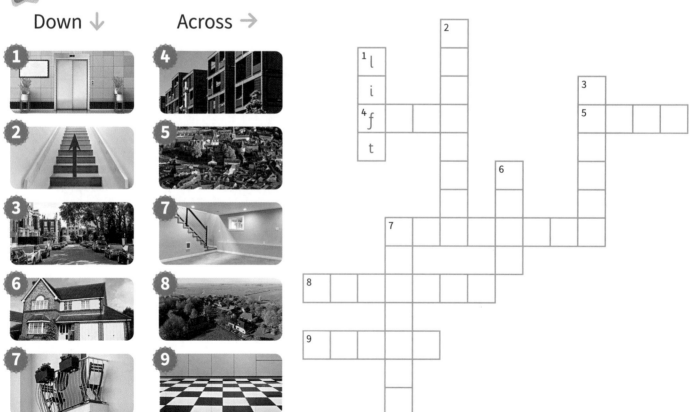

1 ¹l
i
⁴f
t

2

3

5

6

7

8

9

Do the online activities on **Practice Extra** as you complete this unit

Read and complete.

downstairs   ~~village~~   upstairs   floors   balcony   street

Lenny lives in a (1) _____village_____ in the country. There are five houses in his

(2) _____ . His house has got three (3) _____ . Lenny walks

(4) _____ to his bedroom because there isn't a lift. The living room and the

kitchen are (5) _____ . His house hasn't got a (6) _____ , but it's got

a beautiful garden.

 Write about your home. Draw or take a photo.

I live in a _____

_____

_____

_____

Do you live in a village?   No.

Has your house got a balcony?   Yes.

1 Look at the photos. Read and circle. Write number '1' or '2' in the box.

1 The woman is taking / (carrying) a lamp. ☐ 2

2 The girl is carrying / going the box up the stairs. ☐

3 The man is sitting on / carrying the chair. ☐

4 The man is smiling / taking because he's happy. ☐

5 There are boxes in / on the floor. ☐

6 The man is coming in / going out of the door. ☐

2 Read and complete. Match.

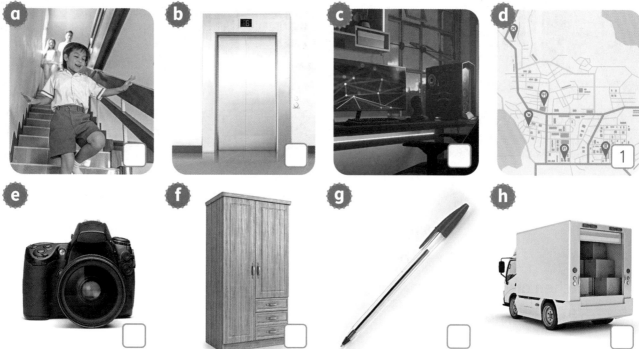

1 We want to find our friend's street. We need a ____map____ .

2 He's eighty and can't climb the stairs. He needs to use the _____ .

3 She wants to write her address on the letter. She needs a _____ .

4 You want to clean your room and put your clothes away. You need
   a _____ .

5 I want to take a photo of my bedroom. I need a _____ .

6 They want to move house. They need a _____ to take their beds and
   cupboards to their new home.

7 He wants to play his new computer game. He needs his _____ .

8 He wants to go to the basement. He needs to walk _____ .

1 Match the words and numbers.

1	90	_twenty_	ewttyn
2	18		ifytf
3	40		etrhinet
4	17		txisy
5	50		niyten
6	60		tihgeeen
7	20		ofytr
8	13		neevnetes

2 Read and colour.

I live at number 83 and my balcony is grey. The balcony above mine is green. The balcony below mine is blue. The balcony at number 95 is red. The balcony between number 93 and the red one is purple. The balcony next to number 73 is orange. There's a pink balcony above the orange one. The balcony next to the orange one is yellow. The balcony at number 85, above the yellow one, is brown.

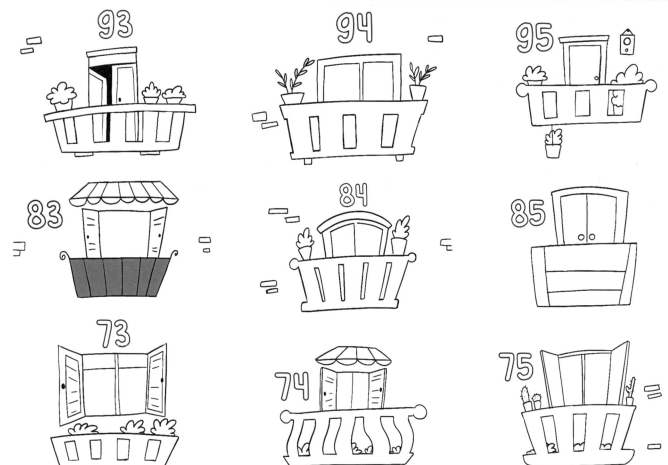

Lock's sounds and spelling

1 **Look and write the missing letters.**

b_ee_   cit____   thirt__n   twent____

sh__p   countr____   sevent__n   sevent____

thr____   tr____   str__t

2 **Read and write the house numbers.**

13

We live in a crazy street. The first house is number thirteen – yes, that one on the left. Three houses along, with the big circle window, is number eighteen. The last house in the street is number three. Next to number thirteen is house number twenty. In between house number twenty and house number eighteen is number seventeen. Next to number three is number forty. That's it – our street!

Movers Reading and Writing

1 🐵 Read the text and choose the best answer.

Charlie is talking to his friend Lily.

Example

Charlie:	What are you looking at?
Lily:	(A) I'm looking at a photo.
	B I can't find my book.
	C Yes, I am.

Questions

1 Charlie: Is this your house?
  Lily:
    A   Yes, in a flat.
    B   No, thanks.
    C   No, it's this one.

2 Charlie: Do you like living in a village?
  Lily:
    A   Yes, you do.
    B   Yes, I love it.
    C   No, I like football.

3 Charlie: Have you got a garden?
  Lily:
    A   Yes, we have.
    B   No, we can't.
    C   Yes, we aren't.

4 Charlie: Is your aunt wearing a grey jacket?
  Lily:
    A   No, it's my favourite colour.
    B   Yes, she is.
    C   Yes, it's blue.

5 Charlie: Is there a shop next to your house?
  Lily:
    A   No, I don't like shopping.
    B   Yes, forty-three.
    C   Yes, there is.

6 Charlie: Do you enjoy taking photos of your family?
  Lily:
    A   Yes, please.
    B   Yes, I like it a lot.
    C   No, a banana.

How are our houses unique?

Practise **Match the words and the contractions.**

1 it is   a I'm
2 we have   b they're
3 they are   c it's
4 I am   d there's
5 there is   e we've

Plan **Reread the description on Pupil's Book page 25. Complete the table.**

	Bethany	My dream bedroom
colours	¹ _____ blue _____ walls	
features	a big ² _____ a lot of ³ _____ a slide a spiral staircase a bed for the ⁴ _____	

Write **Write about your dream bedroom using your notes from Activity 2.**

Edit 4 **Did you ...**

☐ describe your dream bedroom?
☐ include colours and features?
☐ use contractions?

Writing tip
Give your description a title: 'My dream bedroom'.
Begin with 'In my dream bedroom'.

Do you remember?

1 **Read and complete the table.**

Jack lives in a flat in a city. His flat's got a balcony, but it hasn't got a garden. He can play in the basement below his flat.

Mary lives in a very big house in a village. Her house has got a garden and a basement, but it hasn't got a balcony.

Sally lives in a small flat in a city. Her flat hasn't got a basement or a garden, but it's got a beautiful balcony with lots of flowers.

Paul lives in a city. His house hasn't got a balcony or a basement, but it's got a small garden with an apple tree.

	city	village	flat	house	garden	balcony	basement
Jack							
			✓				
						✗	
		✓					

2 **Write the answers.**

1 Where are Lock and Key in the first picture?

2 Why does Mrs Potts ask Lock and Key to go to the basement?

3 How does Key feel when he goes to the basement?

4 What happens in the basement?

5 Why are Lock and Key scared?

6 Why is Mrs Potts smiling at the end?

1 🎧 7 Listen and write the numbers.

1 | 2 | 3
4 | 5 | 6

(1 shows **68**)

2 Read and match.

1 I've got short, straight, grey hair.

2 I've got a black beard.

3 I've got long, black hair.

4 I'm wearing a hat and I've got curly hair.

5 I've got fair hair and a beard.

 a (1)
 b
 c
 d
 e

Circle the odd one out and say.

Granddaughter, grandson and parents are family words.

1 (down)	granddaughter	grandson	parents
2 quiet	clever	balcony	naughty
3 daughter	son	uncle	monster
4 village	basement	town	city
5 fair	curly	straight	thirty
6 street	hair	beard	moustache
7 door	climb	window	wall
8 mirror	telephone	lift	lamp
9 house	shop	home	flat
10 above	between	behind	listen

 Complete the crossword using the words from Activity 3. Use the code to write the message.

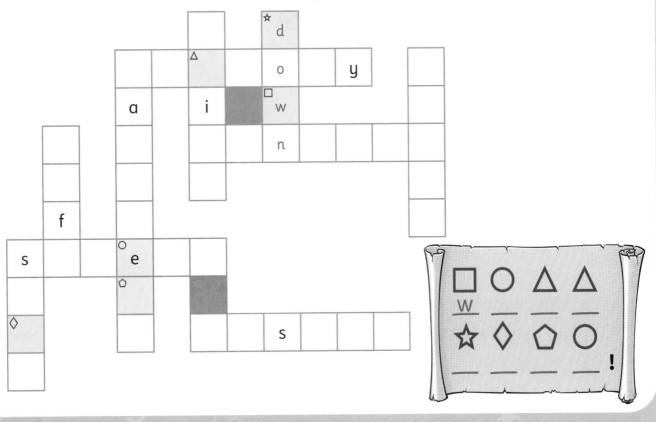

3 A day in the life

1 Read and number the sentences.

Hello. My name is Alisha. I wake up early at seven o'clock. Then I get up and I have a shower. After that I get dressed and go downstairs to have my breakfast. I love breakfast! After breakfast I go to school. My school starts at nine o'clock. I have lunch at school with my friends. School finishes at three o'clock and I go home. I have my dinner, then I do some homework and watch TV before bed. I go to bed at nine o'clock.

a I have a shower. ☐
b I get up. ☐
c I go to bed. ☐
d I have dinner. ☐
e I have lunch. ☐
f I wake up. 1
g I have breakfast. ☐
h I go to school. ☐
i I get dressed. ☐

2 Look and read and write.

Example: The door in the big room is _____ open _____ .

Complete the sentences.

1 The man with the beard is getting _____ .
2 The _____ with curly hair is getting up.

Answer the questions.

3 What is the man with the moustache doing? _____
4 What is the time on the clock? _____

Now write two sentences about the picture.

5 _____
6 _____

   Vocabulary: daily routines | **Language:** present simple   ▶ Do the online activities on **Practice Extra** as you complete this unit

1 Look and match.

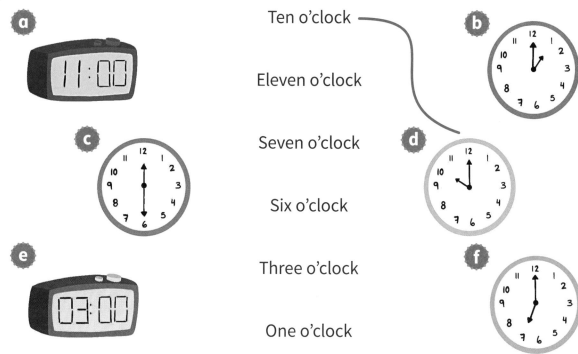

Ten o'clock

Eleven o'clock

Seven o'clock

Six o'clock

Three o'clock

One o'clock

2 Write 'before' or 'after'.

1 I take off my clothes _____before_____ I have a shower.
2 I wash my hands _____ I have lunch.
3 I take off my shirt _____ I take off my jacket.
4 I put on my socks _____ I put on my shoes.
5 I go to bed _____ I have dinner.
6 I get dressed _____ I go to school.

Now write two more sentences.

7 _____

8 _____

3 Talk to your friend. Is your routine the same or different?

Do you get dressed after breakfast?

Do you have a shower before bedtime?

Yes, I do.

No, I don't.

Different! I get dressed before breakfast.

Same!

Find and write the words.

e	f	n	j	a	m	i	h	f	t
a	m	b	i	s	o	c	p	l	h
s	t	u	t	c	n	k	a	o	u
s	a	t	u	r	d	a	y	u	r
u	a	l	e	b	a	n	k	l	s
n	r	g	s	c	y	l	a	w	d
d	h	d	d	e	i	h	a	k	a
a	y	x	a	f	r	i	d	a	y
y	i	d	y	l	s	w	b	a	m
w	e	d	n	e	s	d	a	y	a

M o n d a y
T _____
W _____
T _____
F _____
S _____
S _____

 Look, read and write.

_____ _____ _____ _____

Monday _____ _____

1 Peter always plays basketball after school on Mondays.
2 On Tuesdays Jim and Sally play badminton after school.
3 Jack and Mary do their homework after school on Wednesdays.
4 Daisy has a swimming lesson on Thursdays. She never watches TV.
5 Clare and Fred watch TV with their mum on Friday evenings.
6 Paul goes to the shops with his dad on Saturday mornings.
7 Vicky plays football on Sundays. She sometimes scores a goal.

Vocabulary: days of the week | **Language:** present simple and adverbs

1 Use the words to make three sentences.

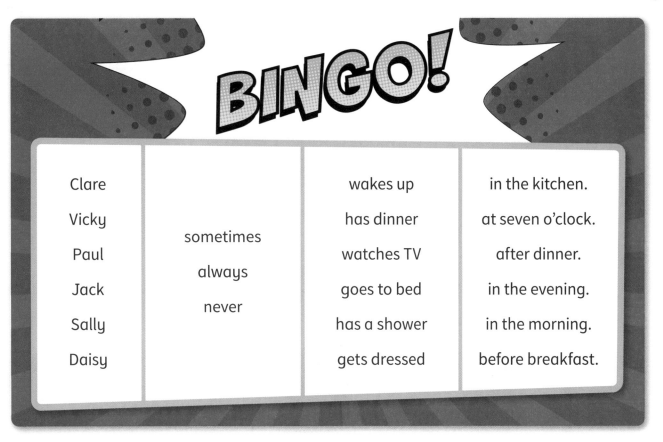

Clare		wakes up	in the kitchen.
Vicky		has dinner	at seven o'clock.
Paul	sometimes	watches TV	after dinner.
Jack	always	goes to bed	in the evening.
Sally	never	has a shower	in the morning.
Daisy		gets dressed	before breakfast.

Now play bingo.

Clare	never	has a shower	in the kitchen.

2 Write sentences about you.

I wake up at _____ o'clock every day. _____

_____

_____

_____

3 Tell your partner. I wake up at six o'clock every day.

Lock's sounds and spelling

1 Say and write.

| wakes up gets up
catches puts on
brushes washes
dances eats
watches | **-s**

wakes up | **-es**

catches |

2 Read and match.

plays ~~gets up~~ catches the bus dances starts school
washes her hands wakes up brushes his hair puts on clothes

1

gets up

2

3

4

5

6

7

8

9

Sounds and spelling: /iz/, /s/, /z/

Movers Listening

1 🎧 8 🐵 **What food does Lily have in these places?**
Listen and write a letter in each box. There is one example.

pancakes [H]

banana [ ]

sandwich [ ]

ice cream [ ]

sweets [ ]

cake [ ]

What do astronauts do in space?

  Look and complete the times.

3.00	9.30	4.00	6.30	10.00	8.30

_____ half four _____ _____ half

o'clock _____ _____ o'clock _____

nine six _____

2 **Reread the blog on Pupil's Book page 35. Which activity does Sally do?**

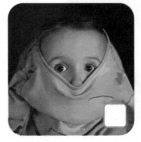   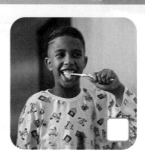 

put on pyjamas go to sleep wash brush teeth

Plan

 Tick (✓) the activities that you do in the evening. Add one of your own.

Write

4 📝 **Write a blog post about your evening routine.**

Edit

5 **Did you …**

- ☐ include your evening activities?
- ☐ include times?

Writing tip

To begin your blog, write the date: 24 June.
Put your activities in order.

Do you remember?

1 Read and complete the story.

On Mondays Paul wakes up at ⏰ (1) _eight o'clock_ . He gets up and

always has a 🚿 (2) _____ . Then he gets dressed and goes to the

(3) _____ for breakfast. After breakfast he puts on his

(4) _____ and he goes to the bus stop to catch a

🚐 (5) _____ . He never walks to 🏠 (6) _____ .

At 🕐 (7) _____ Paul comes home and does his homework before

dinner. After dinner he sometimes plays on his 💻 (8) _____ .

He goes to 🛏 (9) _____ at ⏰ (10) _____ .

2 Write the answers.

1 What does the reporter say about detectives' routine?

_____

2 What time do Lock and Key usually get up?

_____

3 Why aren't Lock and Key at the detective agency?

_____

4 What adjectives are used to describe Lock and Key?

_____

5 Do you think these are the correct words to describe them?

_____

6 Does the reporter think that Lock and Key work a lot? Why (not)?

_____

4 In the city

1 Sort and write the words.

1	rpssot ecnert	4	ukeesrmrpta	7	biduglin	10	toleh
2	wtno	5	enicam	8	aelivlg	11	oshclo
3	lhpsotia	6	ubs ttasoni	9	rac rpka	12	ylrrbia

1. s p o r t s ▪ c e n t r e
2. w
3. i
4. m
5. m
6. ▪ i
7. n
8. g
9. ▪ p
10. o
11. o
12. l

2 Look at the code. Write the secret message.

26	25	24	23	22	21	20	19	18	17	16	15	14
a	b	c	d	e	f	g	h	i	j	k	l	m
13	12	11	10	9	8	7	6	5	4	3	2	1
n	o	p	q	r	s	t	u	v	w	x	y	z

T h e r e's / __ / _____ / ____ /
7 19 22 9 22 8 / 26 / 8 4 18 14 14 18 13 20 / 11 12 12 15 /

_____ / __ / ___ / _____ .
13 22 3 7 / 7 12 / 7 19 22 / 24 18 13 22 14 26

Vocabulary: places   ▶ Do the online activities on Practice Extra as you complete this unit

Look, read and write. Match.

1 You go there to buy food and drink.   supermarket

2 You go there to sleep.

3 You go there to play tennis and volleyball.

4 You go there to get money.

5 You go there to watch films.

6 You go there to catch a bus.

7 You go there to swim and you wear a swimsuit.

8 You go there to buy good fruit and vegetables.

2 Complete the picture. Answer the questions.

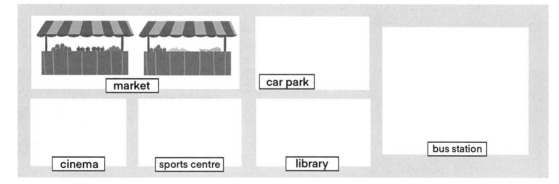

1 Where's the market?   The market is next to the

2 Where's the bus station?

3 Where's the cinema?

4 Where's the car park?

5 Where's the sports centre?

6 Where's the library?

1 Read and circle the best answer.

1 You must be quiet in a

   a) sports centre   (b) library   c) park

2 To catch a bus you must go to the

   a) cinema   b) bus station   c) hospital

3 You must clean

   a) the market   b) the bus station   c) your bedroom

4 To fly your kite you must go to

   a) the supermarket   b) the library   c) the park

5 You must sit down in the

   a) market   b) swimming pool   c) cinema

6 To see a doctor you must go to a

   a) hospital   b) car park   c) market

7 You must take money to a

   a) park   b) supermarket   c) library

8 To see a film you must go to the

   a) cinema   b) swimming pool   c) sports centre

Please be quiet

2 Read and match.

Suzy must tidy her bedroom. She must put the books in the bookcase. She must put her kite on the cupboard and her T-shirt in the cupboard. She must put her crayons on the desk next to the computer and her shoes under the bed. She must clean her desk. She must put her toy box between the bed and the bookcase.

1  **Read and tick (✓). Listen and check.**

At school we must:

answer the teacher's questions ✓

listen to the teacher ☐

wear trousers ☐

run in the playground ☐

come to class with a pencil ☐

eat our lunch in the dining room ☐

put our hands up to speak ☐

sit next to our friends in the library ☐

do our homework ☐

drink in the playground ☐

speak English in class ☐

2 **Write. What must/mustn't you do in these places?**

the library school home	must mustn't	clean my room run respect my teachers help my parents speak loudly

At home I must clean my room.

_____

_____

_____

_____

Lock's sounds and spelling

1 **Complete with 'ere', 'air' or 'ear' and number the pictures.**

1 A big b _ear_ with long h_____.

2 Wh_____ is my ch_____? It's next to the b_____.

3 Look at those apples and p_____s in the market.

4 Th_____ is a b_____ sitting on my ch_____.

2 **Look and write.**

-ere	-air	-ear
where		

1 Look at the small _bear_ sitting on the very big _____ holding an apple and a _____.

2 The big _____ sitting on the very big _____ is wearing a dress.

3 _____ are two _____ on the small _____.

4 There's one _____ with long brown _____ and one _____ with short purple _____.

5 _____ is the _____ on the stairs going?

6 _____ is a _____ behind the _____ on the stairs!

Movers Reading and Writing

1 🐵 **Read the story. Choose a word from the box. Write the correct word next to numbers 1–5. There is one example.**

My name is Jack. I'm ten years old and I live in a house in a small ___village___ .

Behind my house there's a big (1) _____ . I go there with my (2) _____ Bonny. Bonny enjoys going there very much. She loves running and catching a ball. I like going there after school. I play with my friends.

My school is in a big city near the village. I must catch a bus to school, but I can (3) _____ to the bus stop. It's next to my house!

I enjoy going to the city on Saturdays, too. I always go shopping with my mum. We go to the big (4) _____ between the sports centre and the library. We buy our food for the week there.

After shopping I sometimes go to the library to get a good (5) _____ to read.

Example

village

walk

dog

ice cream

supermarket

book

park

climb

school

---

(6) Now choose the best name for the story.
Tick (✓) one box.

Jack's dog ☐

Jack's week ☐

Jack's school ☐

Where do we go shopping?

1 Circle the nouns. Use red for people, green for places, and blue for things.

(Brooklyn) Superhero Supply Company

New York City, USA

Are you a superhero? Do you want to be one? This shop has got superhero costumes, such as masks and capes. You can also buy fun toys and science kits to make things! You can build a robot or write a secret message with invisible ink.

Plan

2 Reread the adverts on Pupil's Book page 43. Complete the table.

Shop name	Moving [1] ___Books___	[2] _____	My shop: _____
Location	different places	[3] _____	
What can you buy?	[4] _____	ice cream	
Why is the shop special?	It can go to different [5]	[6] _____	

Write

3 Make a sign and write an advert for your own shop.

Edit

4 Did you ...

☐ include the location?

☐ include things you can buy at the shop?

☐ say why the shop is special?

Writing tip

Write the name of your shop in big, bright colours! Use capital letters in your shop name.

Do you remember?

1 Put the words in groups.

~~granddaughter~~ ~~hotel~~ ~~upstairs~~ ~~wake up~~ uncle basement cinema daughter
have lunch parent shop stairs get up hospital balcony library
lift grandson catch play aunt café wash downstairs

Actions	Places	Home	Family

wake up	hotel	upstairs	granddaughter

2 Write the answers.

1 What are Lock and Key doing on the computer?

2 What do you think Key is thinking in picture 2?

3 Why is the woman in the green T-shirt smiling in picture 3?

4 Where are Lock and Key going to go? Why?

5 What happens at the bank?

6 Why is the woman in the green T-shirt angry in picture 6?

Review Units 3 and 4

1 **Read and order the words. Make sentences.**

1	play tennis	on	I sometimes	Wednesdays.
2	7 o'clock.	wakes up	Tom never	before
3	at	Mary never	the weekend.	rides her bike
4	before	dinner.	wash our hands	We always
5	do their homework	in	the evening.	Jim and Peter never
6	Sunday mornings.	read	on	They always

1 I sometimes play tennis on Wednesdays.

2 _____

3 _____

4 _____

5 _____

6 _____

2 **Find the words.**

Now answer the questions.

How many town words are there? _____

What are they? _____

_____

Circle the odd one out and say.

Car, lorry and bus are transport words.

1 car	lorry	bus	(feet)
2 lunch	shower	breakfast	dinner
3 afternoon	school	teacher	homework
4 Monday	Saturday	bedtime	Friday
5 always	funfair	sometimes	never
6 library	cinema	stairs	market
7 brother	teacher	mother	father
8 children	between	behind	above
9 evening	morning	afternoon	Tuesday
10 never	get up	wash	wake up

 Complete the crossword using the words from Activity 3. Use the code to write the message.

5 Fit and well

1 **Look and write the words.**

| ear | tooth | back | stomach | ~~head~~ | foot | hair |
| eye | mouth | shoulder | nose | hand | leg | arm |

1 head
2
3
4
5
6
7

8
9
10
11
12
13
14

2 **Complete the sentences.**

temperature   toothache   stomach-ache   ~~cold~~   headache   cough

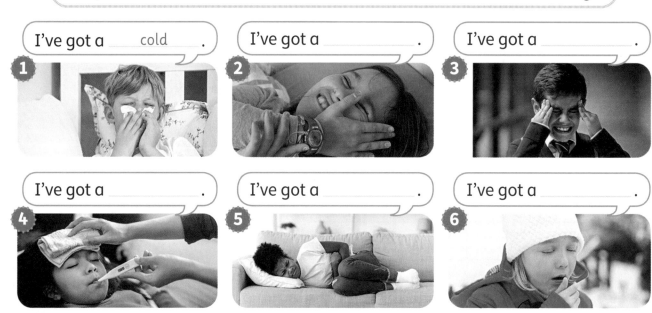

1 I've got a ____cold____ .

2 I've got a _____ .

3 I've got a _____ .

4 I've got a _____ .

5 I've got a _____ .

6 I've got a _____ .

Vocabulary: health | **Language:** *have got* and *has got*   Do the online activities on **Practice Extra** as you complete this unit

Read and circle.

1 My (eye) / leg / ear hurts. I can't read.

2 My toe / back / tooth hurts. I can't eat.

3 My shoulder / foot / finger hurts. I can't kick the ball.

4 My leg / ear / eye hurts. I can't ride my bike.

5 My nose / mouth / arm hurts. I can't play tennis.

6 My foot / hand / knee hurts. I can't catch the ball.

 Look at Activity 1. Write.

1 What's the matter?

My eye hurts.
I can't read.

2 What's the matter?

My _____ .
I can't _____ .

3 What's _____ matter?

4 What's the _____ ?

5 What's _____ ?

6 _____ ?

Language: *What's the matter? My (eye) hurts. I can't (read).*   47

10 **Listen and write the number.**

2

Choose a place and write the rules.

_____

_____

_____

_____

_____

_____

_____

_____

Language: _must_ and _mustn't_ for obligation

1 Look and match.

You mustn't:

play computer games

go swimming

eat burger and chips

listen to music

eat cakes, biscuits or chocolate

pick up a big bag

2 Now write sentences.

1 When you've got a stomach-ache you mustn't eat burger and chips.

2

3

4

5

6

Lock's sounds and spelling

1 **Look, circle and write. Use ''s' and ''ve'.**

1   He / (They) 've____ got a bad headache.

2   He / We ____ got a headache.

3   We / She ____ got a bad cold.

4   She / They ____ got a temperature.

5   We / I ____ got a cough.

6   They / She ____ got a stomach-ache.

1

2

4

5

6

2 **Match and write.**

| I
He
She
They
We | 've got
's got | a cough.
a cold.
a toothache.
a stomach-ache. |
| | mustn't
must | play outside.
go to the doctor.
go to bed.
eat burgers.
eat sweets. |

1   He's got a cold. He mustn't play outside.

2   _____

3   _____

4   _____

Movers Reading and Writing

1 Look and read and write.

Examples

There are eight _____chairs_____ in the room.

What is the baby doing? _____sleeping_____

Questions

Complete the sentences.

1 The boy has got a cold and is wearing a striped _____ .

2 In the poster, the park is between a library and a _____ .

Answer the questions.

3 What's the man with the black shoes doing? _____

4 Where are the books? _____

Now write two sentences about the picture.

5 _____

6 _____

What remedies do we use?

  1 Look and write the affirmative or negative imperatives.

1 ✗ _____ (run) in the corridors.
2 ✗ _____ (use) your phone in the exam.
3 ✓ _____ (write) your name on the paper.
4 ✓ Please _____ (raise) your hand to answer.
5 ✗ Please _____ (eat) in the library.

Plan **2 Reread the leaflet on Pupil's Book page 53. Complete the table.**

	Remedy for the hiccups	Your remedy for _____
Illness facts	• when you're ¹ _____ or when you eat too ² _____ • come from muscle movements	• _____ • _____
Do	• Hold your breath and ³ _____ to ten. • ⁴ _____ sugar or honey.	• _____ • _____
Don't	• Don't worry.	• _____

Write **3 Write about an illness and a remedy. Use the information from the table in Activity 2.**

Edit **4 Did you …**

☐ include facts about the illness?
☐ include dos and don'ts?

Writing tip

Use a title: 'Help! I've got …'.
Write short, clear sentences.

Do you remember?

1 **Read and order the words. Make sentences.**

1	go swimming	Fred can't	ill.	because he's
2	sleep	mustn't	in class.	We
3	got a temperature.	stay in bed	Vicky must	because she's
4	Daisy mustn't	got a backache.	because she's	carry big bags
5	must	We	with toothpaste.	clean our teeth
6	with	the matter	What's	Jack?

1   Fred can't go swimming because he's ill.

2

3

4

5

6

2 **Write the answers.**

1   What does the woman want Lock and Key to do?

2   What's the matter with the man in the painting?

3   Why can't Key decide what to eat?

4   What cakes has Key got?

5   What's the matter with Key?

6   Where is the painting at the end of the story?

6 In the countryside

 1 **Look at the picture. Sort and write the words.**

1 virer _____river_____
2 ldfei _____
3 soreft _____

4 nplta _____
5 keal _____
6 flae _____

7 sgasr _____
8 tfwaleral _____
9 orkc _____

2 **Read the text. Write 'yes' or 'no'.**

The Stars enjoy going to the countryside for picnics. They park the car and walk to the river near the waterfall. Stella loves looking at plants and their leaves and drawing them in her notebook. Suzy enjoys playing on the grass. Simon loves swimming in the lake and walking in the forest with his map. Grandpa loves fishing in the river and sleeping on a towel or a blanket after lunch.

Dotty loves running in the fields, but she must always stay with the family because sometimes there are other animals.

1 The Stars don't like going to the countryside for picnics. _____no_____
2 Stella loves looking at bikes. _____
3 Stella draws plants and their leaves. _____
4 Suzy enjoys playing on the rocks. _____
5 Simon loves swimming in the lake. _____
6 Grandpa loves swimming in the river. _____
7 Dotty loves sleeping in the fields. _____
8 Sometimes there are animals in the fields. _____

Do the online activities on **Practice Extra** as you complete this unit

Ask your friend. Complete the questionnaire.

Free time questionnaire

1 Do you enjoy going to the countryside?

yes ☐ no ☐

2 How often do you go on picnics?

every weekend ☐ sometimes ☐ never ☐

3 What do you sit on when you're in the countryside?

the grass ☐ a towel ☐ a blanket ☐

4 How often do you go fishing?

every weekend ☐ sometimes ☐ never ☐

5 Do you enjoy walking in the forest?

yes ☐ no ☐

6 Do you like climbing trees?

yes ☐ no ☐

7 How often do you go swimming in rivers or lakes?

every weekend ☐ sometimes ☐ never ☐

8 Do you like looking at plants and flowers?

yes ☐ no ☐

2 **Look at Activity 1. Write about your free time.**

In my free time I enjoy going

I   go on picnics

I like

1 Find the pairs and number the pictures.

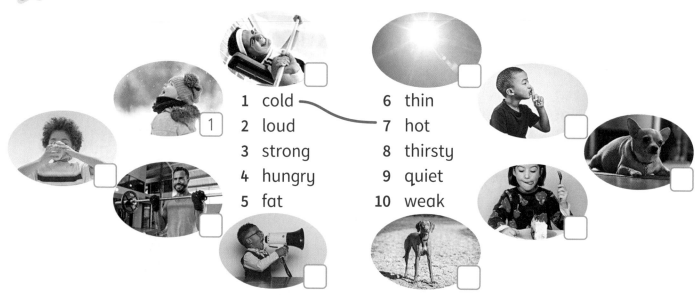

1	cold	6	thin
2	loud	7	hot
3	strong	8	thirsty
4	hungry	9	quiet
5	fat	10	weak

 2 Look and read. Then number and write the questions.

Shall I get a blanket? [1]   Shall I make lunch? [ ]   Shall I get a chair? [ ]

Shall I get you an ice cream? [ ]   Shall I get you a drink? [ ]

1 — I'm cold.

Shall I get a blanket?

2 — I'm tired. I need to sit down.

3 — I'm hot.

4 — I'm hungry.

5 — I'm thirsty.

Vocabulary: adjectives | **Language:** *Shall I …?*

Put the words in groups.

good   hungry   thin

~~weak~~   strong

Words to describe people	Words to describe people and places
weak	

bad   hot

fat   loud

thirsty   quiet   cold

 Look and read. Correct the sentences.

1 Jack wants to drink some water. He's hungry.
   No. He's thirsty.

2 May's got a headache. The music is quiet.

3 Look at Peter. He's very weak!

4 Fred doesn't like the film. It's very good.

5 Anna needs to eat. She's thirsty.

6 Jim's wearing a jacket and a hat. It's hot today.

Lock's sounds and spelling

1 Write the words. Draw lines to match.

> grass   thirsty   four   river   three   bread   crocodile
> rats   forest   ~~grapes~~   parrots   hungry   water

1 g r a p e s

2 _ _ _ _ e _

3 f _ _ _ e _ _

4 g _ _ _ _ s

5 _ _ _ _ _ d

6 _ _ i _ e _

7 _ _ _ _ _ _ d _ _ _ _

8 f _ _ _ _ _ h _ _ g _ _ _ _ t

9 _ h _ _ _ t _ _ s _ _ p _ _ r _ _ s

2 Match the sentence halves.

1 The crocodile wants   a about grapes.
2 The parrots are   b the bread in the river.
3 Three rats are thinking   c to eat bread.
4 The parrots   d drinking water.
5 The crocodile is between   e are in front of the forest.
6 The crocodile mustn't throw   f the grass and the river.

Movers Reading and Writing

1 🐵 **Look and read. Choose the correct words and write them on the lines. There is one example.**

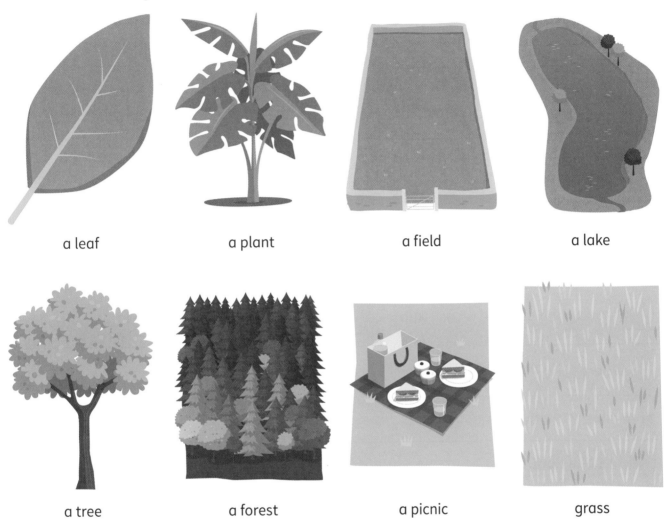

a leaf

a plant

a field

a lake

a tree

a forest

a picnic

grass

Example

This is usually green. You must water it every day.   a plant

Questions

1 This is on the ground. It's green and sheep eat it.

2 We sometimes eat this in the countryside.

3 This is the name for a lot of trees in the countryside.

4 Apples grow on this.

5 You can see horses or cows here in the countryside.

6 This is part of a plant or a tree. It's often small and green.

Why do we live in different places?

1 **Read and circle the words that need a capital letter.**

Hi (jessica,)

How are you? My family now lives in tokyo, japan! It's a very big city. I love it here. I have a new pet – a kitten! Her name is milly. Isn't she cute?

Take care,

ambar

Plan **2** **Reread the emails on Pupil's Book page 61. Complete and write notes for you.**

	Ruby	Metin	Me
Where I live	¹ Australia, countryside	² _____	_____
Free-time activities	riding horses	³ _____	_____
What I like about where I live	⁴ _____	there's lots to do	_____
What I don't like about where I live	doesn't see her friends	⁵ _____	_____

Write **3** **Use your notes to write an email to a friend.**

Edit **4** **Did you ...**

☐ use an opener and closer for your email?

☐ use capital letters for names?

To open an email, use:
Dear (Ruby),
Hi (Metin),

To close an email, use:
Please write soon!
Take care,

Do you remember?

1 🎧 11 **Listen, colour and write.**

2 **Write the answers.**

1 Where are they going for a picnic?

_____

2 What is in the picnic box in picture 4?

_____

3 What is Mrs Potts taking a photo of?

_____

4 Why is Key giving Mrs Potts a blanket?

_____

5 Why does Key want to catch a fish in the river?

_____

6 Why does Key go for a walk up the mountain?

_____

Review Units 5 and 6

1 **Choose your adventure.**

Come to | Treetop Mountain / Coolwater Lake | . Here you can go | swimming / climbing | so remember

to bring | strong shoes / a swimsuit | . You can see | beautiful birds / fantastic fish | and you can walk

| in dark forests / on clean beaches | . It's hot and sunny so you must bring | a hat / water | .

You mustn't | catch animals / fish | here.

Remember to bring your | map / bag | and have fun!

2 **Look at Activity 1. Write.**

My adventure

Come to ...

Here you can go ...

3 **Circle the odd one out and say.**

1 temperature	cough	cold	(shoulder)
2 hungry	sleep	eat	play
3 eyes	hurts	ears	arms
4 stomach	headache	backache	toothache
5 lake	river	sea	field
6 leaf	loud	good	bad
7 run	swim	climb	fat
8 grass	plant	picnic	flower
9 hungry	grass	thirsty	tired
10 loud	weak	quiet	blanket

> Temperature, cough and cold are illnesses.

4 **Complete the crossword using the words from Activity 3. Use the code to write the message.**

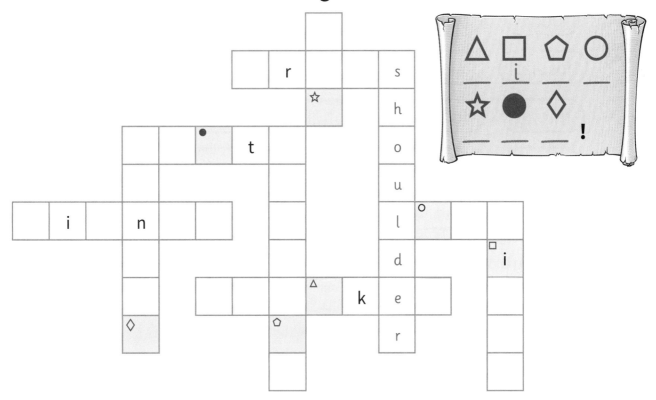

7 World of animals

1 **Put these animals in alphabetical order.**

   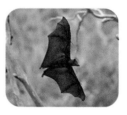 

1 _____bat_____   4 _____   7 _____

2 _____   5 _____   8 _____

3 _____   6 _____   9 _____

2 **Follow the animals. Answer.**

Start →

bear	panda	kangaroo	lion	library	funny
hospital	clean	strong	whale	hungry	fish
thirsty	dolphin	elephant	giraffe	clever	tiger
long	jellyfish	cinema	huge	mouse	bat
naughty	shark	monkey	parrot	hippo	market

Finish →

How many animals are there? _____

There are four city words. What are they? _____

_____

There are nine adjectives. What are they? _____

_____

Look at the animals. Read and correct.

1   This animal has got two legs and a lot of hair on its feet. It eats chocolate and sleeps a lot. It's a big dog.

This animal has got four legs

2   This big green animal lives in Africa. It's got two short, weak legs and two short, fat arms. It can fly. It carries its picnic in a bag next to its head.

3   This big purple or yellow animal can fly but it isn't a bird. It eats ice cream and small cakes. It dances in the day and wakes up and sings at night.

 Write about your favourite wild animal.

My favourite wild animal is

Read and circle.

1 Kangaroos are smaller / (bigger) than bats.

2 Crocodiles are shorter / longer than lizards.

3 Parrots are quieter / louder than mice.

4 Horses are quicker / slower than cows.

5 Giraffes are shorter / taller than hippos.

6 Bears are stronger / weaker than monkeys.

 Look at the picture. Read and write 'yes' or 'no'.

1 The bear's cleaner than the monkey.   yes

2 The bear's sadder than the monkey.

3 The bear's hungrier than the monkey.

4 The monkey's hotter than the bat.

5 The monkey's dirtier than the bear.

6 The bat's happier than the monkey.

1 Read and match. Write the words in the table.

1 strong ⬚ j
2 hungry ⬚
3 good ⬚
4 dirty ⬚
5 clean ⬚
6 bad ⬚
7 weak ⬚
8 fat ⬚
9 easy ⬚
10 thin ⬚
11 quiet ⬚
12 hot ⬚

a cleaner
b easier
c dirtier
d weaker
e hungrier
f thinner
g quieter
h worse
i hotter
j ~~stronger~~
k better
l fatter

long**er**	big**ger**
stronger	

happ**ier**	different!

2 Colour and write.

1 The yellow lion's younger than the red one.

2 _____

3 _____

4 _____

5 _____

6 _____

Lock's sounds and spelling

1 **Think and complete the words with the letters in the box.**

> ph   f   ff   gh

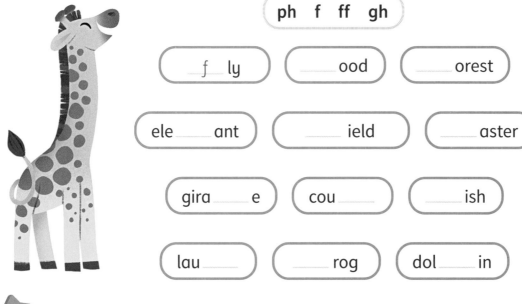

| _f_ ly | ____ood | ____orest |

| ele____ant | ____ield | ____aster |

| gira____e | cou____ | ____ish |

| lau____ | ____rog | dol____in |

2 **Look, read and write 'yes' or 'no'.**

a   The animals are in the city.
   _no_

b   There is a flamingo next to the elephant.

c   The elephant is holding a banana.

d   There's a dolphin in the river laughing.

e   The fish in the river are swimming.

f   There's a giraffe in a T-shirt laughing.

g   The frog is painting a picture.

Movers Listening

1 🎧 12 🐵 **Listen and write. There is one example.**

Charlie's school project

When?		Wednesday
1	How many animals?	
2	Which kind of animals?	
3	Charlie's favourite animal:	
4	Favourite animal's food:	
5	Name of project:	

How do animals stay safe?

Practise

1 **Circle the adjectives.**

1 Sea turtles have got (hard) shells.
2 Grasshoppers have got big legs.
3 Monarch butterflies are orange and black.
4 Hummingbirds have got bright colours.

Plan

2 **Reread the imaginary animal description on Pupil's Book page 71. Complete the table.**

	The hippoctopus	Your imaginary animal
Combination	1 _____hippo_____ , octopus	
Colours	2 _____ , 3 _____	
Safety	The big 4 _____ scare away sharks.	

Write

3 📝 **Write a description of your imaginary animal.**

Edit

4 **Did you ...**

☐ include a name?
☐ describe its colours?
☐ say what it can do?
☐ say how it stays safe?

Writing tip

Illustrate your description.
Do the words match the picture?

Science: animals staying safe | 🛡 creativity

Do you remember?

1 Sort and write the words.

1 tberet   b _etter_ _____

2 geibgr   b _____

3 tedirir   d _____

4 ireeas   e _____

5 rodle   o _____

6 rtqiuee   q _____

7 lsalmre   s _____

8 gonsterr   s _____

9 sower   w _____

10 tefart   f _____

2 Now find the words.

r	d	u	j	m	o	l	d	e	r
b	i	g	g	e	r	r	t	g	e
m	r	x	w	p	m	j	i	q	a
s	t	r	o	n	g	e	r	u	s
e	i	e	r	t	q	f	a	i	i
b	e	i	s	p	w	p	v	e	e
x	r	o	e	u	m	i	a	t	r
s	m	a	l	l	e	r	b	e	o
s	j	q	f	a	t	t	e	r	n
b	e	t	t	e	r	a	g	b	s

3 Write the answers.

1 What's the matter with Lock and Key in picture 1?

_____

2 Why are Lock and Key going to the café?

_____

3 Who is Robin Motors and what does he look like?

_____

4 Why does Key think that it isn't Robin Motors sitting at the table next to them?

_____

5 How is the man at the next table different from Robin Motors?

_____

6 What happens at the end of the story?

_____

8 Weather report

1 Match. Write the words.

a cloud

the sun

wind

a rainbow

snow

rain

1 It's strong.   _wind_
2 It's hot and yellow.   _____
3 It's wet.   _____
4 It's cold and white.   _____
5 It's beautiful and has got lots of colours!   _____
6 It's white, grey or black.   _____

2 Read and circle the correct word.

1 It's hot and (sunny) / snowing. I can wear my swim shorts!
2 It's wet and sunny. There's a beautiful windy / rainbow.
3 It's very grey and cloudy / sunny today.
4 I can make a snowman. There's a lot of snow / sun.
5 We can't go out to play. It's wet and grey. It's raining / sunny.
6 Let's go to the beach. It's a beautiful sunny / windy day.
7 It's snowing / raining in the jungle.
8 It's a beautiful day. It's dry / wet and sunny. Let's have a picnic!
9 It's wet and cloudy. It's raining / rainbow.
10 It's snowing / rainbow in the mountains. We're excited!

Vocabulary: weather   ⬇ Do the online activities on Practice Extra as you complete this unit

 13 Listen and draw the weather.

a · b · c · d · e · f

 Now complete the sentences.

1 In the mountains *it's windy.*
2 In the city _____ .
3 In the forest _____ .
4 At the lake _____ .
5 In the countryside _____ .
6 At the beach _____ .

1 Read and complete the sentences.

wasn't   ~~was~~   sweater   gloves   were   weren't   was   scarf   brilliant

Last weekend, Meera (1) _____was_____ in the mountains with her family.
They (2) _____ on holiday. There (3) _____ a lot of snow.
It was (4) _____ ! Meera (5) _____ cold because she was wearing
a hat and a (6) _____ and she had a (7) _____ under her coat.
Everyone was wearing (8) _____ so they (9) _____ cold.

2 Look at the code. Write the secret message.

26	25	24	23	22	21	20	19	18	17	16	15	14
a	b	c	d	e	f	g	h	i	j	k	l	m
13	12	11	10	9	8	7	6	5	4	3	2	1
n	o	p	q	r	s	t	u	v	w	x	y	z

We / _____ / _____ / _____ / _____ / _____ / _____ .
4 22 / 4 22 9 22 / 18 13 / 7 19 22 / 17 6 13 20 15 22 / 15 26 8 7 / 4 22 22 16

_____ / _____ ' _____ / _____ / _____ / _____ / _____ /
18 7 / 4 26 8 13 ' 7 / 4 22 7 / 26 13 23 / 4 18 13 23 2 / 26 13 23 /

_____ / _____ ' __ / _____ . / _____ / _____ / _____ .
4 22 / 4 22 9 22 13 ' 7 / 24 12 15 23   / 18 7 / 4 26 8 / 21 6 13

---

74   Vocabulary: clothes | Language: past simple – *was* and *were*

1 **Choose two more times and write answers for you. Then ask and answer.**

> Where were you on Monday afternoon?

> I was at the sports centre.

> at home   at a friend's house   at school   at the cinema   in bed
> at the library   in the park   at the shops   at the sports centre

	Me	Friend 1	Friend 2	Friend 3
Monday afternoon				
Tuesday evening				

2 **Write about your weekend.**

On Saturday morning I was

On Saturday evening

On Sunday morning

Lock's sounds and spelling

1 **Circle the correct letters and complete the words.**

1 Every d__ay__ we want to pl____ by the river in the forest. ai / (ay) / ey
2 We love flying our kite when it's sunn____ and wind____. ay / ie / y
3 The ____unny ____ish like to ____ly. f / ff / ph
4 The b____s and the sh____p usually sl____p in the field. ii / ee / ei
5 The bear with purple h____ is sitting on a ch____. ere / ear / air
6 The frog cou____ed and lau____ed at the same time. ph / gh / ff

2 **Read and complete.**

> stomach-ache / headache   bees / spiders   sheep / sleep   ~~sunny~~ / cloudy
> doing / going   jumps / dances   elephant / giraffe   must / mustn't

It's a lovely (1) ____sunny____ day and everyone is out enjoying the warm
weather. Look, there's a cake and the (2) ____ are eating it – oh dear!
The (3) ____ are tired – look they're all sleeping in the field. In the lake
the frog (4) ____ and the flamingo splashes around. The farmer has got his
yellow umbrella with him – where is he (5) ____ ? The (6) ____ is
painting the giraffe as he dances. Oh dear – the rats have got a (7) ____ .
They (8) ____ eat any more!

Sounds and spelling: *y, ee, r, s, ff, ere, air, es, ear, ai, gh, f*

Movers Reading and Writing

1 **Read the text. Choose the right words and write them on the lines.**

The weather

Example	The weather ___changes___ at different times of year. When
1	there _____ a lot of grey clouds in the sky it often rains.
2	When it's raining and sunny, we can sometimes see _____
3	rainbow. Rainbows are very beautiful _____ they have
	lots of colours. Sometimes you can see two rainbows in the sky. When it's
4	hot and sunny _____ people enjoy going to the beach.
	They go swimming and have picnics. But in some countries it gets very,
5	very hot and people _____ go outside in the afternoon.
	In the mountains it often snows when it's very cold. There is always snow
	on the top of some very big mountains.

Example	change	changes	changing
1	are	is	am
2	a	the	an
3	but	or	because
4	both	every	many
5	aren't	don't	haven't

What does nature sound like?

Practise

1 Complete the table.

a-birthday-party   a concert   after school   at 7 pm   at my house
at the park   at a restaurant   a game night   on Saturday

What?	Where?	When?
a birthday party		

Plan

2 Reread the invitation on Pupil's Book page 79. Complete the table.

You're invited!

Come to our nature sounds concert! You can hear musical instruments that sound like thunder and rain. Make your own instruments, too!

Date: Saturday, 14th May

Time: 4 pm

Place: Kyle's garden

RSVP: Please message us on 0786547112 to let us know you're coming. See you on Saturday!

Kyle and friends

		Your event:
Event	A nature sounds 1 _____ concert	
Date	2 _____ , 14th May	
Time	at 3 _____	
Place	Kyle's 4 _____	
RSVP	0786547112	

Write

3 Use the information in Activity 2 to write an invitation to an event.

Edit

4 Did you ...

☐ include the type of event?

☐ include key information about the event?

Writing tip

Invitations usually start with the expression 'You're invited!'

Do you remember?

1 **Write about your day. Draw a picture.**

Yesterday I was _____ with my _____ . There were

a lot of _____ . It was _____ and _____ .

It was fun. I was wearing my _____ and _____ .

_____

_____

2 **Write the answers.**

1   Why does Lock want to go to the police station?

   _____

2   Why are Lock and Key walking in the rain?

   _____

3   Where do they think Robin Motors was on Thursday morning?

   _____

4   Why do Lock and Key think that?

   _____

5   The police officer doesn't agree with Lock. Why not?

   _____

6   Why is Key happy and Lock angry at the end of the story?

   _____

1 **Read, colour and draw.**

Look at the animals. On the island there are two bears. The bear with the fatter stomach is brown and the other bear is grey. Can you see the snakes? The green snake is longer than the yellow one. In the cave there are two bats. The black bat is smaller than the grey bat. There are two birds in the trees. They're parrots. The red parrot is louder than the yellow parrot.

There are two whales and two jellyfish in the sea. The blue whale is bigger than the black and white whale. The pink jellyfish is happier than the purple jellyfish.

There's a boat near the island. Draw a man in the boat. He's wearing a coat and a scarf. He's very hot. The man is looking at the fruit in the trees on the island. He's hungry.

Circle the odd one out and say.

> Penguin, shark and whale are sea animals.

1 penguin	shark	(panda)	whale
2 kangaroo	rainbow	shark	lion
3 wind	snow	rain	beach
4 dry	scarf	sweater	coat
5 parrot	bat	bear	bird
6 wet	hat	cold	dry
7 sunny	dirty	windy	cloudy
8 weaker	better	weather	hotter
9 easier	worse	thinner	teacher
10 raining	countryside	mountains	beach

Complete the crossword using the words from Activity 2. Use the code to write the message.

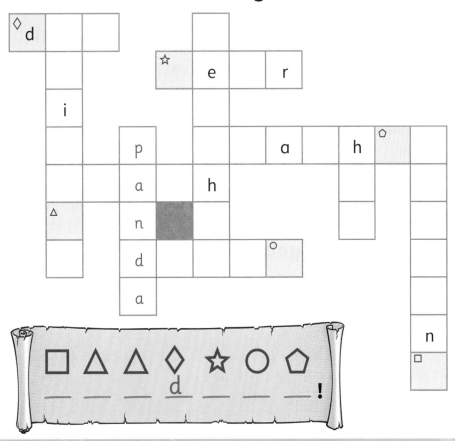

1 🎧 14 **Listen and number.**

a

b

c  1

d

e

 2 **Read and choose.**

1 You've got some toys. You don't want them. Do you:
   a) Ask for some more new toys?
   b) Throw them out of the window?
   c) Give them to the hospital?

2 Your friend wants to play with your game. Do you:
   a) Share your game?   b) Say 'no'?   c) Break the game?

 3 **Think. Write about how you can share what you have with others.**

Units 3&4 Values Love your city

1 Read and choose. Match.

1 You mustn't throw your rubbish out of the door / (window).
2 Where can we park / lift the car? Look! There's a space.
3 Would you like some help / water to get up?
4 Please step / don't step on the flowers.
5 We can / can't play football next to the flowers. Let's play over here.

 2 🎧 15 Listen and check.

 3 Look at the photos and write what is good for the town and what is not.

It's good to help old people on the bus.

_____

_____

_____

1 🎧 **16** **Listen and number.**

1

2 **Complete. Choose the right answer.**

> like   win   help   hurts

1 You _____ . Well done!
  a) Yes, I'm a great player.
  b) Thank you. You're good at tennis, too.

2 Ow! My leg _____ .
  a) Do you want to play football?
  b) Can I help you? Shall I get the teacher?

3 Would you _____ to jump with me?
  a) Oh, yes please! I love jumping.
  b) No. I like to read.

4 Shall I _____ you?
  a) Yes, please. Thanks very much!
  b) No, I don't want your help.

Units 7&8 Values Help the world

1 **Read and match.**

1 Use public transport.
2 Turn the water off when you wash your hair and brush your teeth.
3 Take your bags with you when you go shopping.
4 Walk or cycle to school.
5 Turn electrics off when you aren't using them.
6 Don't use single-use plastics.

 What I can do to help the world.

Grammar reference

Match the sentences.

1 What's Stella doing?
2 What are you doing?
3 What's Simon doing?
4 Is Lenny eating?

a Yes, he is.
b He's kicking a ball.
c She's riding her bike.
d I'm reading a book.

1 Read and circle the best answer.

1 Ben **likes** / **like** reading books.
2 Anna doesn't **enjoy** / **enjoys** having a bath.
3 Grandma **want** / **wants** to ride her bike.
4 Mum doesn't **want** / **wants** to wash the dog.

2 Look and complete.   got   Has   it's got   hasn't

Tom: (1) _____ your new house got a balcony?
Vicky: No, it (2) _____ got a balcony, but it's (3) _____ a basement.
Tom: Has it got a garden?
Vicky: Yes, (4) _____ a big garden for my beautiful plants!

3 Match the sentences.

1 What do you do before dinner?
2 What time does Peter get dressed?
3 How often do you have homework?
4 What does Jim do after school?

a Every day.
b He sometimes plays in the park.
c He gets dressed at 8 o'clock.
d I always wash my hands.

4 **Read and order the words. Make sentences.**

1 (buy food?) (do you) (go to) (Where)

2 (you go) (to) (Where do) (fly a kite?)

3 (you go to) (Where) (see a) (doctor?) (do)

1 _____

2 _____

3 _____

5 **Look and complete.** (mustn't Can must Must)

1 _____ I clean my shoes, Mum? Yes, you must.

2 You _____ listen to the teacher.

3 _____ I run in the playground? Yes, you can!

4 We _____ play tennis in the library.

6 **Match the sentences.**

1 I'm cold.   a Shall I get you a drink?

2 I'm hungry.   b Shall I get you a blanket?

3 I'm thirsty.   c Shall I make dinner?

7 **Complete the sentences.**

1 Horses are _____ than cows. (quick)

2 Sharks are _____ than whales. (small)

3 Bats are _____ than parrots. (dirty)

4 Dolphins are _____ at swimming than whales. (good)

8 **Look and complete the sentences.** (wasn't was were weren't)

On Saturday I (1) _____ at the beach with my family.

It (2) _____ hot and sunny, it was cold and windy!

There (3) _____ many children on the beach.

Where (4) _____ you on Saturday?